T0052574

Johann Sebastian Bach

Six Sonatas for Flute and Keyboard

Edited and realised by

William Bennett

Book Two

WARNING: The photocopying of any pages of this publication is illegal. If copies are made in breach of copyright, the Publishers will, where possible, sue for damages.

Every illegal copy means a lost sale. Lost sales lead to shorter print runs and rising prices. Soon the music goes out of print, and more fine works are lost from the repertoire.

Chester Music

PREFACE

The six **Flute Sonatas** of J.S. Bach (BWV 1030-1035) are thought to date from the Cöthen period (c. 1717-1723) and they fall neatly into two groups of three. In. Nos. 1-3 the composer provided a *concertante* keyboard part where the right hand is as musically important as the flute and bass lines, apart from the occasional passage where he reverts to a figured bass. Nos. 4-6 are for flute and *basso continuo* (i.e. the keyboard part consists of a figured bass only). The two sets also differ in structure: Nos. 1-3 are generally more forward-looking in style and have three movements each (fast-slow-fast)*; Nos. 4-6 adopt the four-movement pattern favoured, for instance, by Telemann.

In recent years the authenticity of **No. 4** has been called into question mainly on stylistic grounds, and it was excluded from the *Neue Ausgabe Sämtliche Werke*. The source for this work is a manuscript in the hand of Carl Philipp Emanuel's chief copyist in Hamburg; in the absence of any definite alternative authorship I see no reason to disagree with its ascription to Johann Sebastian.

Nos. 5 and 6 each exist in several manuscripts, but none is in Bach's hand. A copy of No. 6 was apparently taken by the composer to Potsdam for King Frederick the Great; it is believed that it is due to this visit that the work has survived.

In this edition I have provided the flute part with practical phrasing and dynamics to suit modern performance. This occasionally differs from the manuscript sources; indeed, my belief is that the slurrings in No. 6 were interfered with by a 19th century violinist on the way to the *Bach Gesellschaft* edition, leaving them totally unsuited to performance on the flute. In order to facilitate comparison, the 'original' is shown in the cue-line printed above the keyboard part.

In the keyboard part editorial additions are shown in [ ] and slurs as ⌢⊹⌢ , and the editorial realisation of the figured bass in Nos. 4-6 is printed in full size for the sake of clarity. Dynamics are almost entirely mine; the ones which occur in the manuscripts are identified by footnotes. The original dynamics in No. 4 (iv), bars 37-38 and 83-84 pose a problem: I feel that they are totally ineffective in performance and offer my own solution on the flute part.

William Bennett
London, 1983

---

* I maintain that the first movement of No. 1 should be taken rather more quickly than the marking *Andante* suggests.

SONATA No. 4

J.S. Bach
BWV 1033

I

* *All dynamics in this sonata are editorial.*

† *In the B.G. edition the semiquavers are slurred ♩♩♩♩ until bar 9 iii inclusive.*

© Copyright for all Countries 1983, 1989

All rights reserved

II

44

III

Adagio

IV

Menuett I

* In the original the keyboard part to *Menuett I* was written out in full,
unlike the rest of the Sonata where the figured bass is realized by the editor.

Menuett II

Menuett I ab initio

SONATA No. 5

I

J.S. Bach
BWV 1034

Adagio ma non tanto

© Copyright for all Countries 1983, 1989

All rights reserved

* The Bach Gesellschaft *has* A♮ , *but*
  the present editor believes A♯ *preferable.*

II

Allegro

III

Andante

* in another source.

IV

Allegro

* Bars 2 and 3: original dynamics.
† Bars 5 and 6: the editor considers that these slurs are unworkable and has omitted them from the flute part.

* Bars 37 and 38: original dynamics (see Preface).

† Bars 35 and 41: *basso continuo* ♩♪ in the original.

* Bars 83 and 84: original dynamics ♩♩ (see Preface).

† Bars 81 and 87: *basso continuo* ♩♩ in the original.

SONATA No. 6

I

J.S. Bach
BWV 1035

† *In this Sonata the slurs in the cue line are taken from the* Bach Gesellschaft *edition. The present editor believes them to be mainly unauthentic and offers his own solution in the part (see Preface).*

* *Another possible interpretation:*

© Copyright for all Countries 1983, 1989

All rights reserved

II

Allegro

* Bar 4 and 8: original dynamics.

* Bar 60: original dynamic.

* Bar 64: original dynamic.

III

Siciliano

IV

Allegro assai

† Bar 26: *basso continuo* ♪♪ in the original.

† Bar 53: *basso continuo* ♪♪ in the original.